James Aloysius McCallen

Temperance Lectures

Delivered in St. Patrick's and St. Ann's Churches...

James Aloysius McCallen

Temperance Lectures
Delivered in St. Patrick's and St. Ann's Churches...

ISBN/EAN: 9783337259310

Printed in Europe, USA, Canada, Australia, Japan

Cover: Foto ©Lupo / pixelio.de

More available books at **www.hansebooks.com**

TEMPERANCE LECTURES,

— DELIVERED IN —

St. Patrick's and St. Ann's Churches.

A GRATEFUL TRIBUTE

TO FATHER MATHEW'S MEMORY AND WORK,

By REV. J. A. McCALLEN, S.S.,

MONTREAL.

1890.

EXPLANATORY.

At the urgent request of some friends of our Temperance cause in Montreal, and with the approval of the Very Rev. Administrator of the archdiocese, I have consented to the printing and circulation of the two following discourses on Temperance, in the hope that my words may be productive of some spiritual and temporal fruit to my readers. I may also add that these discourses are a grateful personal tribute to the memory and work of the Rev. Theobald Mathew, the greatest apostle of Temperance whom God has ever given to our race. The only condition I have imposed is, that this little pamphlet be sold at the nominal price of five cents per copy, or twelve copies for fifty cents, so as to bring it within the reach of the greatest possible number of readers.

THE AUTHOR.

Imprimatur :

L. D. A. MARECHAL, V.G.,

Administrator,

Montreal, October 31, 1890.

FIRST LECTURE

DELIVERED

IN ST. ANN'S CHURCH

BY

REV. J. A. McCALLEN, S.S.,

On the occasion of the Celebration of Father Mathew's
Centenary by the Irish Catholic Temperance Convention
of Montreal.

October 12, 1890.

*" This day shall be for a memorial to you, and you
shall keep it a feast to the Lord in your generations
with an everlasting observance."*—(Exodus, ch. xii.
14.)

Very Rev. Administrator, My Lord, Rev. Fathers,
Beloved Brethren: We are gathered here to-day to
celebrate the centenary of Father Mathew's birth—
a man raised up by God to deliver our people from
the modern Pharaoh of Intemperance, just as Moses
was selected for the deliverance of the Israelites
from the tyrant Pharaoh of Egypt. It is consoling to
reflect that God approves of such celebrations,
for they serve to make us remember the blessings
which in all times He has deigned to confer by the
ministry of His chosen servants upon the human race.
The world itself, though generally so cold and heart-
less and ungrateful, is not unmindful of the birthday
of its heroes, of the men who, in the dark hours of
the nation's trials, have nobly sacrificed time and
health and talents, even life itself, for the nation's
welfare.

As Catholics, as Irishmen, or sons of Irishmen, as members of our societies of Temperance, we would prove false to our faith, our country and the noble cause which we advocate, were we to fail to celebrate this birthday feast, and to keep it a memorial from generation to generation, with an everlasting observance. However warm our devotion to the cause of Temperance, our efforts in this direction (let us humbly make the confession) pale into insignificance in the presence of the untiring, unselfish and successful labors of the great apostle whom we honor on this day.

Born October the 10th, 1790, ordained a priest on Easter Saturday, 1814, it was on April 10th, 1838, that Father Mathew began the special work of his apostolate. From the hour in which he signed the total abstinence pledge till that of his death, he labored night and day for the success of the cause which he had so much at heart. God crowned his labors as He never before nor since has crowned the labors of any one man in the cause of Temperance.

Ireland, England, Scotland and the United States were the successive theatres of the battles which he waged against drink. Like Peter the Hermit, and St. Bernard, preaching the crusades for the deliverance of the Holy Land from the hands of the infidel, Father Mathew, by his earnest, sincere and enthusiastic preaching of the Temperance crusade, gathered around the banner of Total Abstinence legions of men, women, and even children, who by word and example were to deliver their land from the tyrant Intemperance, who had so long held it in abject slavery. His disciples were to be counted not by tens but by hundreds of thousands, and it is his glory, as I hope it is his crown, that not only was his pledge administered to greater numbers than that of any other Temperance advocate, but that the pledge which he administered was more universally and faithfully observed.

However interesting it might prove to follow the footsteps of Father Mathew as he travelled from city to city and from country to country, conferring the blessings of sobriety on homes made desolate by drink, I shall leave that grateful task to one of the speakers of to-morrow evening's social celebration, and content myself on this occasion with a few words on the cause which Father Mathew advocated, and on the best means of securing its success.

That cause is Total Abstinence. Total Abstinence is the practice of Christian mortification, and as such must prove agreeable to Him who, from the crib to the cross, led a life of mortification and of voluntary suffering for the sins of men, and who has given self abnegation as a characteristic mark of His true disciple. "If any man will come after Me, let him deny himself." We may add that the Total Abstinence pledge faithfully observed is the only infallible remedy against Intemperance. Men of every profession, of every condition of life, and of the highest virtue and strongest will power, have proved victims of the passion of drink, gliding too easily from the use to the abuse of intoxicating liquors.

Let us remember, however, that our cause can never be advanced by exaggeration and at the sacrifice of truth. Though Total Abstinence is an infallible remedy against Intemperance, it does not follow that total abstainers are the only temperate men in the world. Well-meaning Temperance advocates have maintained that the use and sale of intoxicating liquors are in themselves sinful. Neither proposition can be defended by Scripture or by reason. To my mind, such assertions weaken instead of strengthening our cause. It is the abuse, not the use, of any of God's gifts which constitutes sin. The efforts of Temperance men should therefore be directed to the elimination of the abuse of liquor selling and liquor buying, as practised in this city of Montreal. The discussion of this phase of the Temperance question will enable us to place our cause and the true means for making it a success in their proper light.

Our legislators, if they are true to the best interests of their constituents, not only have the right, but are in duty bound to protect us from the adulterated beverages which are manufactured and sold under the name of liquor in the various groceries and saloons of this city. Much of the evil arising from the use of intoxicating drink can be traced to the ingredients which enter so largely into the adulterated liquors sold to our people. How rapidly is not the brain affected, the body diseased, the health shattered, and an irresistible craving created in those who indulge frequently in drink ? Why are our legislators so slow in passing an inspection law in this matter ? * The butcher who disposes of tainted meat, the drug-

---

* Since the above was written, Mr. J. J. Curran, M.P., Q.C., called the attention of the audience present at the social celebration to the fact, that an inspection law regarding the adulteration of alcoholic liquors did exist. " Alcoholic, fermented and other potable liquors sold or offered for sale, shall be deemed to have been adulterated in a manner injurious to health if they are found to contain any of the articles mentioned in the schedules to this Act." (Adulteration Act, 49 Vic., cap. 107 Revised Statutes of Canada, Section 17.) But as the eloquent speaker remarked, the law was practically a dead letter as far as saloons were concerned.

gist who compounds an injurious prescription, the baker who adulterates his food products, are set upon by the law and severely punished. And meantime the saloonkeeper can send men home day after day, mental, physical and moral wrecks, premature victims for the grave, and do this with an impunity which it is simply appalling to contemplate. Why this liberty (might I not say unlawful license) to one class of our citizens which is accorded to no other? Let us then demand a law for the inspection of all liquors manufactured and sold in our city. And let the law be rigidly enforced not only by fines but by imprisonment. It is a just law, and as citizens we claim the right to demand it of our legislators.

Experience having taught that the liquor trade combined with the grocery offers such facilities to wives, mothers, sisters, daughters, to procure intoxicating drink which so often drags them from the high plane on which man's love, respect and veneration have placed them, down to the lowest depths of infamy and degradation, can our representatives at Quebec turn a deaf ear to the appeals so often made to them for a law separating these two trades? Do our legislators really respect womanhood? If so, why not protect it, save it from the blighting, withering influence of the passion for drink? If love for our Temperance cause has no influence with our law makers, let the name of mother, wife, sister, daughter touch their hearts. If we must have drunkards among our men, let it not be said that Quebec and Montreal refused to protect womanhood from this shame. No woman having any self respect will enter a saloon to purchase liquor. To the grocery, therefore, may we trace, as to its legitimate cause, the passion for drink observed alas! in too many of the women in this city. Let us have a law separating the grocery from the liquor trade.

We have a Sunday law. Is it enforced? I would like to say yes. But love for truth makes me say emphatically no! Is it not a crying shame that even the Lord's day must be desecrated by the drunken orgies of so many of our citizens? Can we, as Catholics, look on unmoved at such desecration? Why tolerate this abuse? Why, I again ask, allow the transgressors of the Sunday law to go unpunished? What right has the saloon-keeper or the grocer to have his side door or back gate in such practical use on Sunday, even during the hours of service in church, while other merchants keep their places of business closed? Why do the officers of the law shut their eyes to these infractions of the law? Fines for such infractions are of little avail. Imprisonment for first offence and cancellation of license after third offence will prove a just and successful check to the desecration of the Lord's day which all Christian men so earnestly deplore. One party in this city was convicted seven times in one year of selling liquor on Sunday. He paid fines aggregating $550, and yet never closed his place a single Sunday. We have a Sunday law. And since fines have failed to check the avarice of the Sunday seller, let him be sent to prison. We are a Christian people, a remarkably religious people. Let us see to it that our religious feelings be not outraged by the sight of men under the influence of drink on the Lord's day. Let the saloons be closed from 7 p.m. Saturday till 7 a.m. Monday.

We have a law forbidding the sale of intoxicating liquors to minors. Should it not be rigidly enforced? The clergyman who dares to unite in marriage, without the parents' consent, two parties one of whom is

a minor, will be punished by law. How seldom are
men punished for selling intoxicating drink to minors!
How can any saloon-keeper in conscience deal out
to young people, still in their teens, the liquor that
will blast forever lives so full of promise to the young
themselves and to their country? There is not a
father or mother who gets the breath of liquor from
the lips of a child, but should at once prosecute the
would-be murderers of their boy. As a matter of
fact such prosecutions are rare, and we may therefore
conclude that the law against selling to minors is
little better respected than the Sunday law. We of
the clergy, who are so often brought face to face with
the evils growing out of the unlimited and unchecked
liberty of liquor dealers to sell when and to whom
they please, would fail in our duty were we not to
raise our voice against so crying an abuse. Are there
ten liquor dealers in this city who during the past
twelve months have never sold a glass of intoxicating
drink to a minor or to a well-known drunkard? If
there are, let us have their names, and the promise
that they will forfeit their license if we can prove a
case against them.

Finally—for however practical and useful the sub-
ject which we are discussing may be, I must not
abuse your patience—finally, then, have we not in
the best interests of our people the right to require a
diminution in the number of 'saloons' of this city?
Two classes of persons object to this reduction. On
the one side, the Government, because, say they, " our
revenue will be diminished "; on the other the saloon-
keeper, because, say they, " you unjustly rob us of our
means of a livelihood."

To the members of the Government, I reply: Re-
duce the number of saloons, but impose a higher

license tax so as to double your revenues. It has
been done elsewhere. It certainly might at least be
tried in Montreal. Philadelphia in 1887 had nearly
six thousand saloons for its million of people. Now,
for more than a million of people, it has only 1300,
and yet by raising the tax from $50 to $500 it has
more than doubled its revenue. The exact figures
are: With 4326 less treail licenses granted in 1888
than were issued in 1887 the total receipts were :
For Philadelphia city $534,464; for the State $169,-
100 ; total $703,564, as compared with a total of
receipts in 1887 of $285,680, none of which was paid
to the city. I might add to this the saving in court
and jail expenses, by recalling the fact that in the first
year of high licenses in Phildelphia there were 8,000
less convicts than in the year preceding high license.
And the same is true of many other cities in which
high license has been tried.

Perhaps we are asking too much of our legislators.
May they not pay heavily, five years hence, for their
courage in passing laws restricting the liquor traffic
if the saloon influence should be exerted to rob
them of their seats in the halls of legislation? I cannot believe, I do not believe, that the majority of our
legislators are to be influenced by such fears. And
while there may be a few who dare to sav privately
that the saloon-keepers have stood by them on the
day of election, and they in turn will stand by the
saloon keepers, any politician who would make such
an avowal in one of our daily papers over his own
signature would be at once branded as a hireling and
coward. He certainly would not deserve the name
of a conscientious statesman. Our legislators repre-
sent in Parliament not the saloon-keeper but all the
citizens of their electoral district. These have rights

that must be respected. During five years the seats in Parliament cannot be contested. And if to the mass of citizens, the legislator gives the protection of a high license law and a diminution of saloons in this city, the increased number of sober grateful men will take good care, that their friends in Parliament will not suffer by having followed the dictates of an enlightened conscience, and will return them with increased majorities to the legislature.

But will not higher license prove an injustice to a number of saloon-keepers who will thus be driven out of the business ? Not more so than taxes prove to men of other avocations, who, after a lifetime spent in one business, find themselves, through the taxes imposed upon their plant and upon the products of their labor, obliged to seek another means of livelihood. Not more so than to the property owner, who is obliged by law to abate, at his own expense (sometimes very heavy expense), the nuisance which endanders the health or well-being of his neighbors. Why is it that the saloon-keepers must be always treated as a privileged class ? Do not the great majority of the saloons in this city prove a nuisance to their neighbors by endangering the health, aye, the very life, of both the drunkards, who sally forth from these drinking houses, and the poor victims of the drunkard's fury in the drunkard's own home ?

What is it robs the laboring man of his hard-earned money? Liquor. What is it robs his home of joy and comfort ? Liquor. What is it impoverishes his family ? Liquor. What is it steals away his reason, his strength, his manhood, his self-respect ? Liquor. What crime fills our orphan asylums, our jails, our reformatories? What crime brings so many idlers on our streets ? Intemperance. What crime causes most

tears to flow, most hearts to be crushed, most homes
to be made desolate ? What crime most leads men to
other crimes ? Intemperance. Intemperance begets
impurity, dishonesty, sloth, anger, revenge. What
crime, in a word, robs man so effectually of the
image of his God, and stains his soul with its own
infamy and the infamy of other degrading vices? Intemperance. And in presence of all this woe and
poverty and sin and desolation, brought upon so
many of our citizens by the too numerous saloons and
licensed places of the city, we are told we will com-
mit a great injustice to saloon-keepers, if, by a reduction of the number of saloons, we strive to lessen the
temptations of men who want to be temperate, but are
too weak to fight the battle, with such fearful odds on
the side of the enemy. Legislation to be just, must
consider the needs, the interests of the many, not of
the few. Therefore, let us have fewer saloons, as few
as possible, and let not all of them be located at the
very doors of our laboring people, but scattered at
great distances over the city. Thus only can our
honest men of toil manage to reach their homes
without temptation alluring them from the path of
duty at every step.

O my brethren, awaken from the dreadful apathy
in which the liquor traffic, as practised in Montreal,
has left so many of you, its citizens. In this Father
Mathew's Centenary year, lend us a helping hand in
our efforts to make you a sober, prosperous people.
Let it not be said that while your brethren across the
sea, in your own dear island home, are rallying under
the banner of their bishops and their priests (with
an enthusiasm like to that manifested by their fathers
fifty years ago) to do battle against the demon,
drink; while your brethren in the United States are

making efforts greater than were ever made before to lessen the evils caused among our people by Intemperance ; let it not be said that you alone will be found unworthy children of the great Temperance apostle and Irish priest, Father Mathew, the Centenary of whose birth you are to-day celebrating.

O glorious Apostle of Temperance, if in reward for your life's labors in this grand cause, you have already received your crown, deign to look down upon the people of this fair city, and, touched by the woe and desolation and sin which your eyes behold, pray that we may one and all arise in our might and overthrow the power which has so long enslaved the noblest, the best, the most virtuous of our citizens. Pray that we may have the courage to do as thou hast done, if not for our own protection, at least as an example to the weak and wavering, and in thy very words, to promise with the divine assistance to abstain from all intoxicating drink, and to discountenance the cause and practise of Intemperance. Then indeed will thy birthday be a glorious memorial for us, a true feast to the Lord, to be kept in our generations with an everlasting observance.   Amen.

SECOND LECTURE

Delivered in St. Patrick's Church,

· By REV. J. A. McCALLEN, S.S.

October 26, 1890.

" The ear that heard me blessed me; and the eye
that saw me gave witness to me: because I had deliv-
ered the poor man that cried out, and the fatherless
that had no helper. The blessing of him that was
ready to perish came upon me. I was clad with jus-
tice, and I clothed myself with my judgment, as with
a robe and a diadem." (Job xxix. 11–14.)

BELOVED BRETHREN,—These words of the inspired
text may be most appropriately and justly applied to
the Rev. Theobald Mathew, whose Centenary is now
being celebrated throughout the Catholic world. You
who now listen to me are the children of Irish, Eng-
lish, Scotch, and American parents, to whom Father
Mathew taught the important lesson of sobriety;
while some here present learned the same lesson from
the very lips of this zealous apostle himself, receiving
the pledge at his hands.

However much has already been said of this great
and good man, this benefactor of the human race;
however much may still be spoken and written of
his life and labors, I feel that I would not be true to
his memory and to the cause which he advocated, if,
in this mother-church of the English-speaking Catholics of Montreal, I were to allow his Centenary to pass
without another tribute to this glorious apostle of
Temperance, and to his no less glorious work.

Wherever he journeyed, he found men slaves of drink, bound by fetters which deprived them of all true liberty. He found men who, through intemperance, had become poor, not only in temporal possessions, but poor by the loss of so many spiritual favors which had once enriched their souls. And these men, in their misery, and slavery, and poverty, cried out for a saviour, a deliverer, to hasten and break their fetters and set them free ; cried out for some rich benefactor to come and restore to them the prosperity, temporal and spiritual, of which they had been robbed And when their ears drank in the words of wisdom and justice and virtue which he spoke to them ; when by word and by example he led them to exchange the yoke of the tyrant drink for that sweet yoke of Total Abstinence, sweetened by the knowledge that it was the yoke of Christian mortification, willingly accepted, they rose up free men ; they rose up to walk in the way of prosperity ; they rose up to be once more true Christians ; and they blessed him, and they blessed God who had sent such an apostle to them. And when, as the years rolled by, their eyes beheld the glorious change effected by the practice of sobriety,— their manhood restored, their homes made happy, their self-respect regained, their souls purified,—their eyes bore witness to this change, and their voices proclaimed the debt of eternal gratitude which they owed to Father Mathew, who, by Total Abstinence had brought such priceless blessings to their hearts and homes. The orphans too, often made such by the excesses which had hurried many a father to a premature grave, raised their voices in praise and thanks- giving, that, though fatherless, they still could lean securely on the mother, whose sober Christian woman hood gave them the protection of which Intemperance had in part already robbed them. "*The ear that heard me blessed me; and the eye that saw me gave witness to me, because I had delivered the poor man that cried out and the fatherless that had no helper.*"

Total Abstinence will still effect a similar change in your minds and hearts and homes, if you profit by the lessons which Father Mathew spent his life in teaching.

Oh! how many of all professions, of all conditions of life, of all ages and of both sexes cry out to-day as they did in Father Mathew's time: "*Save us, we perish!*" "*The blessing of him that was ready to perish came upon me.*" Are there no men nor women listening to me who will answer this cry and merit this blessing? Alas, how comparatively few move hand or foot, or raise their voice to help on this noble cause of Temperance, on the success of which, however, depend in great part the morality and prosperity of this city! Will Father Mathew's Centenary year pass by and leave us just where we are; or will the men and women of St. Patrick's congregation, aye, the men and women of this entire city, take our cause to heart, and, exclaiming like the crusaders of old: "*God wills it, God wills it,*" hasten to swell our numbers and insure the victory for which we have so long battled?

Is our cause a just cause? Who will dare deny it? "*I was clad with justice, and I clothed myself with judgment as with a robe and a diadem.*"

We do not ask much of our legislators. We simply ask that they lessen the evils of the liquor traffic, as now practised in this city; that they lessen the temptations which are daily thrown in the way of our people to prevent them leading sober lives.

You are not angels but men; and because you are

men, the alluring pleasures of drink that meet you at every step, prove too much for poor human frailty, and as a necessary consequence many alas ! fall, some never to rise again.

Our cause is a just cause, and every motive that is grand and noble and inspiring—every motive suggested by faith, by charity, by patriotism, appeals to you to make that cause your own.

As Catholics, you should aid the cause of Temperance. Temperance is a virtue, and Total Abstinence is its surest safeguard. What a power for good is not the example of sober Catholics? As Catholics, you are taught that when a man finds by sad experience that the use of intoxicating liquor almost invariably leads him to its abuse, he is bound under pain of mortal sin to fly from this proximate occasion of offending his God. Again, the Catholic Church has ever been the fruitful mother of souls, willing to make a sacrifice of self for the good of their neighbors. There are, of course, amongst us many who, for the sake of their weak and erring brethren, practise total abstinence. But what grand results might not be obtained were their numbers increased a hundredfold or more ! What a strong motive too in favor of Total Abstinence, is suggested by our faith, our love for Christ suffering on the cross ! He underwent the torture of a cruel thirst to atone for the excesses of the intemperance of men. Will not the fervent members of our congregation, the fervent Catholics of this entire city, honor that sacred thirst, and by voluntary mortification of the taste, share in the sufferings of the Man-God, and make a salutary reparation for the numerous sins of Intemperance committed by our people ?

Even as men, the Temperance cause appeals to

all that is noble and best in the human heart. How often do not men, at the risk of their own lives, cast themselves into the rushing torrent of yonder mighty river, in order to save a fellow-creature from a miserable death? Can they look on unmoved at that other mighty torrent of Intemperance, which is fast carrying the best and noblest of our citizens far beyond the reach of human help?

The daily press records with enthusiastic praise and gratitude the daring exploit of the hero who, at the risk of his own life, dashes before the lightning express, as it bears down with frightful rapidity on the unconscious child playing on the track, and gathers its precious little life into his arms, to place it in those of the horror-stricken but now joyful mother. Will there be found no men in our city, no men in our legislature, to at least clog the wheels of that other destructive engine of evil, Intemperance, which threatens the lives of the youths of Montreal? In a word, will there be found men to resent every insult put upon woman except this one of drugging her with liquor, and stamping her fair brow with the infamy of drunken wife, mother, sister or daughter? In certain cities of the United States, a saloonkeeper (and in Montreal we must include the grocer) who dares to sell intoxicating drink to a woman or to a minor has his license at once cancelled. Let the men of Montreal see to it that at least womanhood and childhood be saved from the curse of drink.

Finally, as citizens of Montreal, will not a love for its prosperity, its morality, its fair name, rouse the people to demand wholesome laws for the regulation of the liquor traffic?

What prosperity can come to any city, which allows so many temptations to drink to be put in the way of its working classes ? Is it not a fact of experience that thousands of our working people sink their hard-earned cash in the bank of the gilded saloon, with no other dividend to the unfortunate depositor, except the loss of his money, of his health, of his reputation, and of his virtue ? If the drunkard were the only sufferer we would still have a strong motive for seeking to lessen his facilities for making such investments. But his wife, his children, his home, do not they appeal to us as citizens for help, for protection against this curse?

Visit the night refuges of our city, the winter homes of so many houseless wanderers, and too many of those who seek such shelters will tell you why they are homeless, and why they beg their daily bread. Visit our jail, and many a convict will inform you that but for liquor he would be an honor to his family, and he is its shame; a support to wife and children, and they no longer receive his help; a worthy citizen of Montreal, and he is a foul blot on its fair name. The morality of the city must necessarily suffer from such a sad state of things. There are men in this city, many of them Catholic as well as Protestant, who will tell you that they were faithful husbands and pure citizens till the night of their first drunken debauch. There are men in this city, many of them Catholic as well as Protestant, who will assure you that they never defrauded their neighbor of a penny till liquor demented them, or the craving for liquor urged them to steal that which would purchase drink.

We admit all this, you say ; but what would you have us do ?

I would have you speak, I would have you act. Speak to one another, encourage one another to lessen the evils of which we complain. Speak to the legislator, to the politician, and tell them that you will have, must have, better laws, and laws that shall be enforced. You should also act, not, alas, as you too often do, in favor of the saloon and against the cause of Temperance. Have not many of you by your own signatures encouraged the existence of saloons whose proprietors utterly disregard the Sunday law, the law in regard to minors, and the law of common justice and charity, which should make them refuse drink to well-known drunkards? Why have you not manhood enough to refuse such requests? You tell me these men are your friends, your neighbors, you must treat them with kindness (!) Is the priest not your friend also? Are not his time, his talents, his very life always at your service? Is it not for your sake he foregoes the pleasures of life, the delights of society, and the companionship of his most devoted friends? And meantime, through a false liberality towards the saloon-keeper, you encourage intemperance, which thwarts the best efforts of the priest for the amelioration of his people. Are not your wife, your brothers, your sisters, your children, and other neighbors friends also? Must you, then, to show your friendship to one, two or ten saloon-keepers bring a curse upon a hundred relatives or friends? Give the true reason of your cowardly act, or allow me to give it for you. You too easily sign petitions for liquor licenses, because the backbone of your manhood, if it exist at all, has been broken.

The true way to act, is to refuse to sign a license for every s aloon-keeper, who openly or furtively disregards the laws of God and men. The true way to act towards any man who sells intoxicating drink to your relatives or friends, who abuse it, especially when warned not to make such sales, is to use every legitimate means to drive that man out of the business. The true way to act, is to refuse your signature to every new applicant for a liquor license ; for we have at least ten times too many issued licenses already.

Women too can help and should help in pro-moting the cause of Temperance. Alas, how often has not the downfall of once sober and respected men been traced to woman's weakness in this matter! Is it not possible to have a few gentlemen friends visit your homes without setting before them ale, beer and strong liquors? You call this hospi-tality. What will you call it when these same men, from the depths of an infamous drunkard's life, curse the day that your fair hands extended to them the fatal cup which has brought them to irretrievable ruin? What will you call your alleged hospitality, when these same guests will curse the day that saw them cross the threshold of your homes? Far be it from me to speak lightly of the Gospel virtue of true hospitality. But are there no other refresh-ments to be offered to your friends but ale and beer and strong liquor? Is there no way to entertain your guests than by teaching them the first lesson, or of repeating the lesson already learned, by which they find the most direct and rapid road to mental, physical and moral ruin? Oh! my dear friends, take my warning in time. It is not only the saloon which makes drunkards. Some men never entered a saloon, some men never would have been tempted to enter a saloon, had not the fair hands of women, by extending the fatal cup of intoxicating liquor to their lips, given them the taste for drink, and through that taste caused their future downfall. "But it is their own fault if they abuse my hospitality (?)" Let it be so. It will, nevertheless, remain true, that you could have saved them from the temptation, and you placed temptation in their way. It will, nevertheless, remain true that if they do come to ruin, they will justly lay the blame at your door.

Young ladies can help not only the cause of Temperance, but of noble, sober manhood. Let it be a settled thing among all our Catholic ladies, that any young man who drinks intoxicating liquor will be refused admission to their social gatherings. By such action you will not only elevate and ennoble their characters, but you will secure for yourselves and for others, worthy husbands to love and support you, not lazy drunkards who will look to you for support.

Pardon me, my dear brethren, if I speak thus. Take my place for one month. Stand by the bedside of a man or woman in *delirium tremens;* give daily audience to the poor victims of drink, who beg piteously to be saved from the demon, who is destroying both their souls and bodies; listen to the heart-rending cries for bread from the lips of the drunkard's childdren; visit homes made desolate by drink; hear the sobs, the wailings of broken-hearted wives, mothers, sisters, daughters. And then return here brokenhearted yourselves, because the absence of law or the mal-administration of the laws which already exist have made your hands powerless to save a noble, generous and glorious race. Return here, and take the place which I now occupy; and my words, for uttering which I have just begged your pardon, will seem to you as the far-off echo of the mighty torrent of reproof, indignation and denunciation which will flow from your own lips.

Once more I appeal to you as Catholics, as men, as citizens of Montreal, not to allow Father Mathew's Centenary to ِ pass by, without securing from the Legislature better liquor laws than now exist, and laws that will be maintained in all their majesty, by fines, imprisonment, and cancellation of the license of every offender.

Thus, and only thus, will Montreal promote and defend the noble cause of Temperance. Thus, and only thus, will she deserve, fair city that she is, to take her place among all the cities of the Dominion as their queen, "clad with justice and clothed with judgment as with a robe and a diadem."